Why Doesn't My Floppy Disk Flop?

Why Doesn't My Floppy Disk Flop?

And Other Kids' Computer Questions Answered by the CompuDudes®

Peter Cook

and

Scott Manning

Illustrated by Ed Morrow

John Wiley & Sons, Inc.

New York • Chichester • Weinheim • Brisbane • Singapore • Toronto

Published by John Wiley & Sons, Inc.
Published simultaneously in Canada.

CompuDudes is a registered federal trademark of Peter Cook and Scott Manning.
Design and production by Navta Associates, Inc.

The publisher and the author have made every reasonable effort to ensure that the experiments and activities in this book are safe when conducted as instructed but assume no responsibility for any damage caused or sustained while performing the experiments or activities in the book. Parents, guardians, and/or teachers should supervise young readers who undertake the experiments and activities in this book.

Library of Congress Cataloging-in-Publication Data:

Cook, Peter
      Why doesn't my floppy disk flop? : and other kids' computer questions
  answered by the CompuDudes / Peter Cook and Scott Manning.
         p.   cm.
      Summary: Discusses the history of computers and explains their various
  parts and uses, hardware, software, the Internet, good computer etiquette, and
  their future. Sidebars answer questions asked on the authors' radio show.
      ISBN 0-471-18429-2 (paper : alk. paper)
      1. Computers—Juvenile literature. [1. Computers.] I. Manning, Scott, 1962— .
  II. CompuDudes (Radio show) III. Title.
  QA76.23.C67 1999
  004—dc21   98-42151

Printed in the United States of America

10 9 8 7 6 5 4 3 2 1

Contents

Welcome to Our Book

NO MATTER what you already know about computers, you have something in common with everyone else who uses a computer—you have questions about it! How do we know this? Starting back in 1989 we began appearing on a radio program on WXPN-FM in Philadelphia called *Kid's Corner,* hosted by Kathy O'Connell. Every week kids call us with questions about computers, and we've put many of these questions together in this book.

Say you want to know more about the Internet—just flip to Chapter 3. Have you ever wondered what computers were like in the old days? Some of the answers can be found in the Introduction—plus we have added a bibliography that lists our favorite computer history books. And if you are wondering what the computer world may be like in the future, turn to Chapter 5.

Both of us have been using computers since before the first personal computer was made, and we have used almost every machine at one time or another. We should be able to answer most of your basic questions. If you can, check out our radio show or visit the CompuDudes Web site at http://www.compududes.com.

Introduction
Highlights of Computer History

A VARIETY of inventions from many different cultures contributed to the development of your computer. It took many technological leaps over the last several hundred years to develop an electronic computer that can do all the amazing things your computer can do. And the history of future computers is happening now. It all started with . . .

Calculators

While you may think of a calculator as that battery-powered thing that you use to do your math homework, a calculator is actually any tool used for counting numbers. Your hands are a great calculator for adding and subtracting small numbers, but for more complicated calculations, people had to invent calculating machines.

In 1617 John Napier, a Scottish nobleman, invented Napier Rods to make it easier to multiply and divide. These were sticks with four flat sides that had numbers marked on them. To calculate, you aligned the rods in the right order. From Napier's invention, William Oughtred, an Englishman, invented the slide rule in 1621. To calculate using a slide rule, you slide the numbers printed on it into the correct positions. Twenty-one years later, a Frenchman, Blaise Pascal (for whom the programming language was named), invented an adding machine to help his father, who was a tax collector.

Mechanical Calculators

Two centuries and many inventions later, in 1822, an Englishman named Charles Babbage started to design a mechanical calculator called the "difference engine." Its purpose was to produce mathematical tables to help scientists and businesspeople with their work. Babbage was obsessed with designing the ultimate calculating machine. He put over ten years of work into the design of a huge, complex machine and spent a lot of the British government's money, but he never finished it.

Before this first machine was finished, he was already designing the next one, called the "analytical engine." Neither project was finished when Babbage died. But if you visit London, England, either in person or by way of the Internet, you will find a working difference engine, which was built after Babbage died, at the London Science Museum (you can visit their Web site at `http://www.nmsi.ac.uk/`).

Electric Calculators

One of the most famous electric calculators was designed by Herman Hollerith to help calculate the 1890 United States Census. The Census Bureau collects information about every person living in the United States. In the 1800s processing all the information collected by hand could have taken more than eight years. By that time the information would have been out of date and not very useful.

Hollerith designed a machine that worked with punched cards. Each card contained the answers to all the questions for one person. After all the cards were collected, they were run through the machine and the machine counted all the answers.

The First Electronic Computers

During World War II, the U.S. Army's Ballistic Laboratory, needing help in keeping up with large amounts of calculations, gave the University of Pennsylvania in Philadelphia the task of building the first electronic computer. ENIAC (Electrical Numerical Integrator and Computer) was designed by a graduate student, J. Presper Eckert, and a professor, John Mauchly.

ENIAC wasn't finished until after the war was over in 1945. Although it was used by the military, it was also used to help scientists predict weather and to figure out complex problems in airplane design and nuclear physics.

INSIDE ENIAC

ENIAC was not like your desktop computer. It was eighty feet long and three feet wide. It used eighteen thousand vacuum tubes that had to be changed constantly because they burned out like light bulbs. The Philadelphia newspapers claimed that the computer needed so much electrical power that it dimmed the lights in the city, but that was not true. Parts of ENIAC are on display at the Moore College of Engineering ENIAC Museum at the University of Pennsylvania in Philadelphia, Pennsylvania, and at the Smithsonian Institution's National Museum of American History in Washington, D.C.

Big Mainframe Computers

After World War II Eckert and Mauchly went into business and started the Eckert-Mauchly Computer Corporation in 1948. Their first computer, designed for an aircraft company, was called BINAC (Binary Automatic Computer).

Their most famous computer was the UNIVAC I (Universal Automatic Computer). It weighed sixteen thousand pounds, had five thousand vacuum tubes, and could make about a thousand calculations per second (fast for its day, but computers these days can compute a lot faster). The UNIVAC became famous in 1952 as the first computer to appear on television, when it was used to predict who would win the presidential election between Dwight Eisenhower and Adlai Stevenson. As the computer predicted, Eisenhower was the winner.

Around the same time, IBM (International Business Machines) got into the business of making large computers.

Modern Personal Computers

The microprocessor, or computer chip, is what made the personal computer possible. In 1974 the Intel Corporation created the first central processor chip, known as the "8080," which was used in the first personal computer, the Altair. Since then, Intel has created lots of chips, each one faster than the last one. If you want to see what they look like, stop by the Intel Museum Web site at `http://www.intel.com/intel/intelis/museum`.

Other early personal computers were the Apple II, the Osborne portable computer, the Radio Shack Model I, and the Texas Instruments 99A. They were made in the late 1970s for use at home.

Since then, personal computers have been getting faster, smaller, and more powerful every year, and companies are always making innovations. Some new ideas catch on and others don't last more than a few months. The future home computer will be shaped by what you, as the computer user, decide is a good feature.

People in Modern Computing

The most famous names in modern computing are Bill Gates and Steve Jobs. Bill Gates, along with his college friend Paul Allen, founded the Microsoft Corporation. Bill Gates left Harvard University before he graduated to start the company and develop Microsoft DOS, the first computer operating system for the first IBM personal computer. Bill Gates is one of the richest men in the world. Microsoft makes software that is used on most computers, including Microsoft Windows, Word, Excel, and Microsoft Internet Explorer.

Steve Jobs and Steve Wozniak founded the Apple Computer Company and built one of the first personal computers, the Apple II, in 1977. In 1984 Steve Jobs introduced the Macintosh, which instantly became one of the most popular computers.

FASTER AND FASTER

Every year computers get faster and faster, but did you know that someone predicted this already? His name is George Moore, and his law is called, naturally, Moore's Law. The law says that every two years the speed of the central processor will double.

WHAT IS THE TOUGHEST THING A COMPUTER EVER DID?

A computer doesn't know the difference between hard and easy because it doesn't think. A computer simply does the tasks you give it. But computers do things that humans would find very tough. For example, launching a space shuttle is all done by computer. The computer has to keep all four parts of the shuttle (two booster rockets, fuel tank, and shuttle) plus the five rocket engines working together. Computers also do difficult calculations quickly that would take humans a very long time. For example, ten years before the launch of a spacecraft to Uranus, scientists used a computer to figure out how long it would take the spacecraft to get there. The computer correctly calculated the exact day and time the spacecraft would arrive.

HARDWARE

EVERYONE has a general idea of what a computer is, but not many *really* know what's going on inside that beige box on the desk. But don't worry, it's not as complicated as you may think.

From the largest computer that NASA uses to keep the space shuttle flying to the smallest computer chip inside your microwave oven, all computers do the same three basic things. First, they get information from the outside world. For the space shuttle, that information includes how fast it is going, how high it is, and so on. For the microwave oven, the information might relate to the kind of food you are putting in it. Next, computers do something with that information, like decide how much fuel to burn to move the shuttle, or how long to cook your popcorn. Once that is decided, they send out signals to make the engines burn or the microwaves bounce around in the oven.

The Basics

What are hardware and software?

Hardware refers to all of the parts of the computer, from the computer box to the computer monitor to the printer. Software refers to all of the programs that go into your computer.

What are the basic parts of a computer?

The monitor is the big screen that you look at. The computer box is what holds its guts—all the chips, circuit boards, and so on. The central processing unit (CPU), the chip that carries the basic instructions about how the computer works, is in this box, so people sometimes refer to the box as the CPU even though it contains much more than just the CPU. The box also includes one or more slots, or disk drives. The keyboard is what you use to type words and commands. The mouse is the little box with a rolling ball inside that you use to move the cursor around the screen.

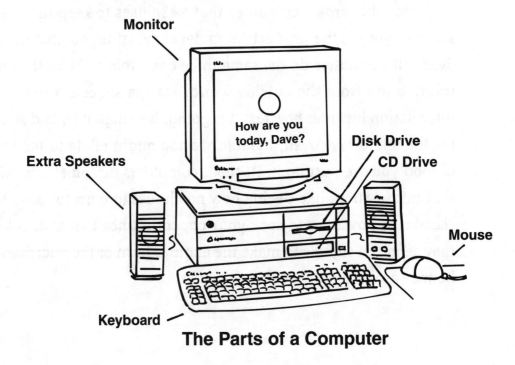

Monitor

How are you today, Dave?

Extra Speakers

Disk Drive

CD Drive

Mouse

Keyboard

The Parts of a Computer

What is a motherboard?

If you look inside a computer, you will see a huge circuit board that fills one side of the case. Circuit boards, computer chips, and wires are all connected together on the motherboard, or the main circuit board, of the computer. The motherboard (there isn't a fatherboard) is where you find the basic circuits like the central processing unit and RAM memory chips. The parts like the sound card, the floppy disk drive, and the CD-ROM player are all connected and controlled by the motherboard.

What is a computer chip?

A computer chip is a tiny group of millions of electronic components and circuits in your computer that make it work. These days computer chips are made of silicon and metals like tin, gold, and copper.

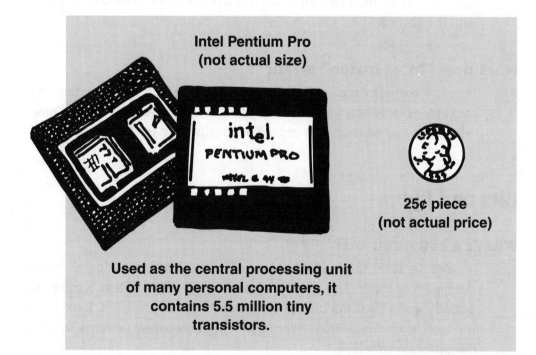

**Intel Pentium Pro
(not actual size)**

**25¢ piece
(not actual price)**

**Used as the central processing unit
of many personal computers, it
contains 5.5 million tiny
transistors.**

What's the point of making things in a computer so incredibly tiny?

There are two reasons why circuits in computers are so tiny. First, if the parts were larger, and they could be, your desktop computer would be the size of your house and you couldn't have laptops or palmtops. The second reason is that the smaller you make computers, the faster they can go. By reducing the length of the wires and the distance between computer chips you actually speed up the computer.

Can you make a computer so small it can fit in your brain?

Not yet, but in April 1998 two doctors from Emory University, Dr. Bakay and Dr. Kennedy, connected a human brain to an electronic device that amplifies brain signals. The signals are transmitted from an antenna connected to the device to a laptop computer. The patient, who is completely paralyzed, is able to move the computer cursor around a screen and communicate with the doctors.

What does "Intel Inside" mean?

Intel is a company that makes computer chips for most of the computers sold in the last twenty years. The Pentium and the Pentium II are very powerful chips that contain your central processing unit or CPU.

Bits and Bytes

What's a computer bit?

A computer **bit** is the smallest unit of data handled by a computer. It represents either 0 or 1. This is known as a **binary** number system. A computer actually works by using on and off switches. If a switch is off, it means 0; if it's on, it means 1. There are millions of microscopic switches within a computer's microchips.

```
111111111
100010001
100000001
110000011
111101111
111111111
```

**Romance writer
April May Grunderungerson
hard at work**

How many bits does a computer use at once?

Your computer works in 8-bit chunks called **bytes.** It also works with 16 bits at a time (called a word) or 32 bits at a time (called a long word). The number of bits that a computer works with depends on what you ask it to do. If you are working with letters, your computer is moving bytes at a time, because one byte can store one character (one letter, or space, or punctuation mark). If you are painting with an art program, your computer will usually work with long words, because 32 bits is enough data to record all of the colors that you can see.

Memory

What is memory?

Memory in a computer is a lot like an address book that the computer uses to keep track of numbers and other information. For a program to run, the computer must load it into memory; then it starts following the instructions one at a time. If the program tells the computer to add two numbers and then multiply that answer by another number, the computer will first do the addition and then store the answer in memory and use it to multiply.

Computer memory is organized as a bunch of addresses, one per byte. The computer can read or write to any address in memory without going through every address before and after it. This is called **random access.**

What is the difference between RAM and ROM?

The most important type of memory is usually called random access memory, or RAM. The name *random access* means that you can get to any storage location that you want in any order. Actually all computer memory is random access. The important thing about data stored in RAM is that it will hang around only while the power is on. If you turn the power off without saving your work somewhere else, you will lose any data that you have been working on.

The other type of memory that you will find in a computer is called read-only memory, or ROM. Like RAM, ROM is random access, but unlike RAM, anything stored in ROM is going to be stored in the computer chip forever. In addition, *read-only* means that you cannot change the data that is stored in ROM; you can only use it. The instructions that tell the computer how to start up and read the hard drive are stored in ROM.

OFF TO A SLOW START

The earliest computers did not have ROM. Instead, when you turned your computer on, it would just sit there and do nothing until you entered the commands to start up, using a row of switches on the front of the computer. It could take an hour of slow switch flipping to get your computer started. And if you made a mistake, you had to start all over again.

How much memory do I really need?

The amount of memory that you have in your computer is very important. When we talk about memory, we mean RAM, or random access memory. If you do not have enough, your computer may run very slowly, or it may not run some programs at all. Figuring out how much memory you need is not an exact science.

As of this writing, most computers have 32 megabytes of memory installed. Computers that people use to create professional three-dimensional graphics have 64 megabytes. The amount of memory that people need has been increasing constantly, and we can only say that sometime in the future you will probably need more RAM.

It's always a good idea to read the side of the box when you buy a new game or other software. All software boxes list how much RAM each program needs to run on a computer. Make sure your computer has enough memory left to run that program.

If your computer's hard drive makes a lot of noise and the little hard drive light on the front of the computer flashes a lot while you are using programs, then it is a good idea to put more RAM in your computer. You will first have to find out how much RAM you have. This can be done by clicking on your computer's control panel and clicking on the Memory area for a Mac or the Device Manager on the Windows PC. Next, if you plan to add more memory, ask your parents to take the computer to a computer store to have new RAM chips installed.

Disks, Drives, and Monitors

What are disks?

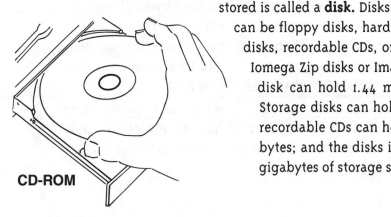

Since RAM forgets everything that is stored when the power goes away, you need somewhere to put your data when you want to turn the computer off. The place where data is stored is called a **disk.** Disks can be floppy disks, hard drive disks, recordable CDs, or backup storage disks like Iomega Zip disks or Imation Super Disks. A floppy disk can hold 1.44 megabytes of information. Storage disks can hold 100 megabytes or more; recordable CDs can hold as much as 650 megabytes; and the disks in hard drives have several gigabytes of storage space.

Hard Drive

CD-ROM

3½ inch Floppy Disk

Iomega Zip Drive Disk

Floppy disks, recordable CDs, and Iomega Zip disks are all portable. They can be inserted into a disk drive in your computer or attached to your computer to collect information, then given to someone to use on another computer. The hard drive uses a hard disk that stays inside your computer.

Floppy disks are the least expensive, but they are not good for permanently storing data. The thin, floppy plastic can wear out and lose data over many years.

Why doesn't my floppy disk flop?

The 3½-inch-wide "floppy" disk you have is covered by a hard plastic case. Inside the protective hard case is a thin piece of plastic that is actually floppy, or flexible. The first portable disks, in the early 1980s, were larger and were enclosed in floppy plastic cases. They could easily be damaged if they were accidentally bent. After people switched to hard plastic cases, the name "floppy" just stuck.

KILOBYTES, MEGABYTES, GIGABYTES, AND TERABYTES

Information stored on a computer's hard drive, on floppy disks, and on backup tapes and disks is measured in bytes. Computer graphics and computer-animated movies like Disney's *Toy Story* can take up hundreds of terabytes. A kilobyte is one thousand bytes, a megabyte is one million bytes, a gigabyte is one billion bytes, and a terabyte is one trillion bytes. Remember that one character takes up one byte of space.

Is there any difference between a hard drive and a floppy drive?

There is one big difference: speed. In a floppy drive the recording head actually touches the disk, but in a hard drive the head flies over the disk. So saving to your hard drive is faster than saving to a floppy disk. To give you a good idea of the speed of your hard drive and how fast the head flies over the hard drive disk, imagine a jet airplane flying along at about 600 miles per hour only 10 inches above the ground. The head of a hard drive flies over the hard drive platter that quickly.

TAKE CARE OF YOUR FLOPPY

One of the things that will always be damaging to a floppy disk, even if it is in a hard plastic case, is a magnetic field. Information is recorded onto a floppy disk using magnets. If you get a floppy disk near a magnet, you can lose the information stored on that floppy disk.

Why does my computer make funny noises when I turn it on?

When you turn your computer on, the hard drive has to start up. The first thing that it does is start spinning the platters inside. This is what makes the whining sound that you hear at first. The next thing that happens is a clicking sound as the hard drive moves the read/write heads back to the outer parts of the platter. These sounds are normal, and you should hear them the same way every time you start up your computer. If these sounds change, you may need to have a service person check things out to make sure that your hard drive is okay and not getting ready to break. You can't see any of this because the hard drive is sealed inside a case. The sealed case keeps out dirt and dust and protects the hard drive platters.

HEAD CRASH!

If you bump your computer while the hard drive is saving something, and the recording head in the hard drive hits the disk itself, you will experience something called a "head crash." This is not something that you ever want to happen to you. If your hard drive head crashes, the head will scrape up the iron coating on the disk and destroy the head and the disk. All of your programs and the stuff you create and store on the hard drive are in that iron coating, so if you damage the iron coating, you will lose everything.

There is no good way to fix a drive after a head crash, but there is an easy way to prevent one in the first place. First, make sure your computer is on a sturdy desk or table, and be sure that it is sitting flat on the desk, not propped against something that might move and let the computer fall.

Also, if you have to move the computer, be sure to wait a few seconds after you turn the power off before you do it. Hard drives can spin for a while after you turn the power off. You want to be sure that everything has stopped before you move the computer.

And finally, if your computer has been in a cold place, let it warm up inside the house for a half hour before you turn it on. The metal and plastic parts in your computer can bend or break if they go from cold to hot too fast.

My hard drive is full. What can I do?

There are three things you can do. First, start cleaning up. Get rid of all those old programs that you never use, clean up temporary files (files that programs use while they run, and are supposed to clean up afterwards, but don't always), and move things like old schoolwork to floppy disks and delete them from the hard drive. Just make sure you know what you are deleting from the hard drive and that you have your parents' permission. You don't want to end up deleting any important instructions to the system or your dad's manuscript!

Second, if you have Windows you can adjust the size of the Recycle Bin, which is located on your computer desktop. The Recycle Bin is where you toss files you want to delete from the computer's hard drive. Place your mouse cursor over the Recycle Bin, and click the right mouse button once. In the little window that appears, click on "Properties," and another window will pop up called "Recycle Bin Properties." In the middle of the window is a slider that selects the percentage size of your hard drive that is reserved for the Recycle Bin. When you buy a new PC, the slider is always set at 10%. This means that if you have a 6.4-gigabyte hard drive, 640 megabytes are set aside for the Recycle Bin. Reset the slider to 1%. You will free up a lot of megabytes this way. You can always change it back if you have to get rid of a huge file.

The third way to get more space is to buy a bigger hard drive. You can replace your small hard drive or even add a second hard drive to most computers. However, a new hard drive costs at least $200, and you would have to pay someone to install it.

What is my computer doing when I first turn it on?

As the computer powers up, you will see information displayed on your monitor. On a PC, numbers and words will fly by. On a Mac, you will not see the numbers during the startup of the computer—you see words that say "Welcome to MacOS," referring to the Macintosh operating system. The computer will check the RAM as well as information about drives and whatever other things are in, or attached to, your computer. A memory chip in your computer called the BIOS (Basic Input/Output System) chip stores all of this information. Once your computer has checked to make sure everything is working, it will display your desktop screen.

This process of starting up is called "booting up," and it comes from the old expression "pulling yourself up by your bootstraps."

Your computer has a lot of work to do before it is ready to do what you want it to. Once the computer is sure that all systems are going, it will look for instructions about what to do next. These instructions are usually part of the **operating system,** a software program that tells your computer how to organize information. The more advanced your operating system is, the longer it will take to start.

How does my monitor work?

Your monitor's screen, like most TV screens, is actually a really big vacuum tube. A **vacuum tube** is a sealed glass container that has all of the air removed from it. In the back of the tube, which is also called a cathode ray tube, or CRT, is a device called an electron gun. This gun fires a stream of electrons at the inside of the front of the CRT. The inside of the glass is coated with special chemicals called **phosphors,** which glow when the electrons hit them. If you have anything that glows in the dark, it has phosphors in it.

But how does the computer control what the electron gun draws on the screen? It's done with magnets. One magnet moves the electron beam stream left and right, and a second magnet moves it up and down, sort of like an Etch-A-Sketch toy drawing screen. When the electrons hit a spot on the screen, the spot glows. That small spot is called a **pixel.** The computer screen can have as many as 1,024 pixels across and 768 pixels up and down. That's a total of 786,432 pixels covering the entire screen.

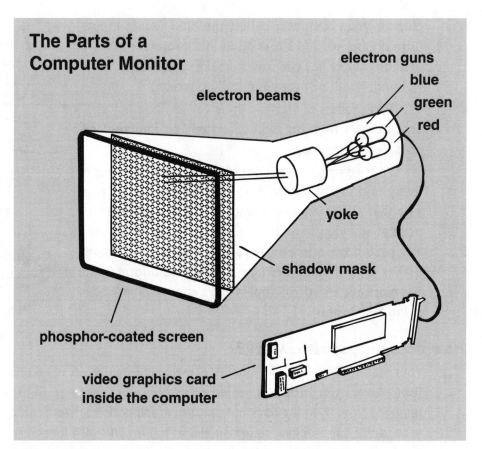

The Parts of a Computer Monitor

electron guns

blue

green

red

electron beams

yoke

shadow mask

phosphor-coated screen

video graphics card
inside the computer

In a color monitor, instead of a single coating of phosphors, the inside of the screen is printed in a pattern of three phosphors, one each for red, green, and blue. Instead of one electron gun, there are three guns, one for each color. Using different combinations of these three primary colors, your monitor can display up to sixteen million colors.

What is a modem?

A modem is a device that allows your computer to communicate with other computers through a telephone line. An internal modem fits into a special slot inside your computer. An external modem plugs into a socket on the back of your computer. A telephone wire is attached from the modem to a telephone jack. The modem changes your data into sounds to send it through the telephone wires, and then another modem on the other end changes the sounds back into data.

Accessories

How do I get to hear sound on my computer?

Your computer may already have speakers and a **sound card** (hardware that sends sounds to the speakers), or you can have them added. The sound card connects to the motherboard inside your computer. The speakers connect to the sound card through a cable in the back of the computer.

I have three speakers attached to my computer—why?

If you have three speakers and one of them looks like a big box, you have a great sound system. The big box is called a **sub woofer**—no, it doesn't bark like a dog. The sub woofer is designed to play the deep bass sounds of explosions, booms, and deep bass voices. The other two speakers send out the high- and middle-range sounds. When you set them up, put the sub woofer on the floor under your computer desk, and place the other two speakers to the left and right of the desk.

What is a CD-ROM drive?

CD-ROM stands for compact disc—read-only memory. The computer CD drive works the same way as the compact disc player attached to your family stereo. Information in the form of sound, graphics, words, and video is stored on the disc—up to 650 megabytes!

The information is read off the disc in a unique way. If you looked at the bottom of the disc (the side without pictures or words) with a very powerful microscope, you would see little pits and scratches in the compact disc. Those pits are information. When the disc spins in the CD-ROM drive, a laser beam flashes on the pits and the computer reads the information off the disc. Be careful not to scratch the bottom of the disc, because that will make the laser beam skip over information.

What is a trackball?

A trackball is an upside-down mouse. The ball and the buttons and some-times a scrolling wheel are located on top. The trackball device stays still while you roll the ball with the palm of your hand or your thumb.

What is a touchpad?

Like a mouse and a trackball, a touchpad is a way to move the cursor around. It looks like a small flat piece of plastic and is sometimes part of a keyboard. Touchpads are often used on laptop computers. All you do is touch the pad with your finger and slide your finger to move the cursor on the screen. On some touchpads you can even tap the pad to open and close folders and files.

What is a track point?

Built into some laptop computers, almost always between the *G* and *H* keys, is a small rubber stick called a **track point**. When you move it around with your index finger, it moves the cursor.

My parents said there are also pointing devices called a hamster and a rat—are they kidding me?

A **hamster** is really a mouse without a cord. Most hamsters, also known as wireless mice, use radio signals to transmit to the computer where the cursor is. A rat is a mouse that you move on the floor with your foot. They are not often used anymore because they are dif-ficult to handle.

What is a joystick?

A **joystick,** which is sometimes plugged into the sound card, is made for playing games. It lets you move something on the screen very quickly in many directions, so it's great for things like flight simulation. A joystick usually has a plastic grip and is attached to a plastic base. Some joysticks have buttons on the stick and on the base that do different things depending on what game you are playing. It might even have a sliding switch that can control speed in something like a car-racing game.

What is a graphics tablet?

If you like drawing pictures on your computer, you can use a mouse or you can use a **graphics tablet.** The tablet comes in sizes from twelve inches wide to nearly three feet wide and it plugs into the computer. You draw on the pad with a pen without ink. As you move the pen across the pad, you will see what you are drawing on the screen. You have to use special graphics software with the pad to create pictures. Some software lets you change what the pen can do. With a simple click, the pen can print a black line or even paint like a brush.

What is a scanner?

A **scanner** is a piece of hardware that lets you electronically transmit printed pictures into a computer. In addition to plugging the scanner into the computer, you will need to load the software that comes with the scanner and allows your computer to reproduce the scanned image. There are two basic types of scanners: A **flatbed scanner** works like a copy

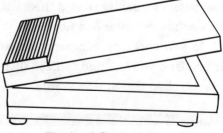

Flatbed Scanner

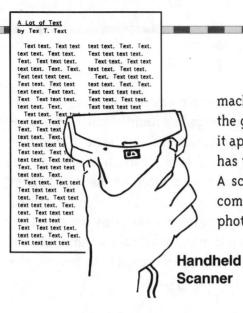

**Handheld
Scanner**

machine. You lift the lid and place a picture on the glass surface. After the picture is scanned, it appears on your screen. A **handheld scanner** has to be dragged across the picture by hand. A scanner can be very useful for creating a computer family album and also for getting photographs onto your Web site.

What is the difference between inkjet and dot matrix printers?

These days most people use an inkjet printer that prints in color as well as black and white. An **inkjet printer** sprays a fine mist of ink on the paper where the computer tells it to.

A **dot matrix printer** is an older kind of printer that works by printing dots to create the shapes of letters. Small pins hit an ink ribbon, and the

SILICON VALLEY

Silicon Valley is located in Santa Clara County, California, about fifty miles south of San Francisco. The valley is a place where hundreds of computer companies have offices and hundreds more have been started in home garages and basements. So many computer companies started there that by 1972 it was nicknamed "Silicon Valley" by electronics writer Don Hoeffler.

In New York City, computer companies call their part of the city "Silicon Alley." In Scotland you can find "Silicon Glen." And across the Midwest, you will find places called the "Silicon Prairie."

dots of ink stick to the paper behind the ribbon. If you look very closely at anything printed on a dot matrix printer, you can see the tiny dots.

What is a laptop computer?

A laptop computer can do the same things as your desktop computer, but it is small enough to fit on your lap, or about the size of a small briefcase. Many people use laptops because they are so easy to carry from one place to another that you can use them almost anywhere. Some laptop cases are made of supertough metal so that even if you accidentally drop them, the laptop will still work. Laptops are usually more expensive than desktop computers because it costs more money to make the smaller parts.

What is a palmtop computer?

A palmtop computer fits in the palm of your hand, and you can carry it around in your pocket. Some palmtop computers can even read your handwriting. A palmtop is so small that a hard drive or a floppy disk drive can't fit inside it. One of the cool things you can do now is check your email by simply plugging a palmtop into a telephone jack.

Why don't they make computers in colors?

Nearly every computer comes in boring colors like white, black, or beige. But now there are some companies like Nokia that make monitors with red, yellow, blue, and green cases. Apple Computer's iMac also comes in several colors. You can also decorate your computer case with stickers, but make sure you don't cover up the floppy disk drive, the CD-ROM drive, or any of the holes or buttons on the case. Also, a few companies, like Nickelodeon, sell cardboard frames that you can attach to your monitor. The frames can be anything from the shape of a TV set to a border of tropical fish to characters from your favorite TV show.

Fun with CD-ROM Discs

You can make your own crafts with CD-ROMs. But first make sure to use CD-ROMs that are demonstration copies or CD-ROMs you get in the mail for online services like CompuServe or America Online. Check with your parents first to make sure that the CDs are never going to be used again.

CD-ROM Mobile

MATERIALS
- String
- Scissors
- 2 metal coat hangers
- Even number of CD-ROMs—4 or 6 (or more)

DIRECTIONS
1. Cut two 12-inch and four 6-inch pieces of string.

2. Attach one end of a 12-inch piece of string to the top of a hanger.

3. Tie a 6-inch piece of string to each corner at the bottom of the hanger.

4. Attach one CD to each 6-inch string.

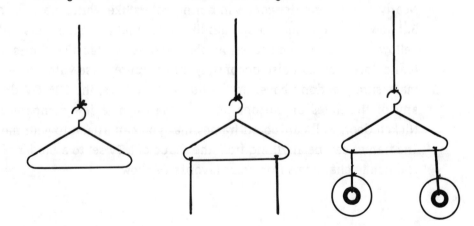

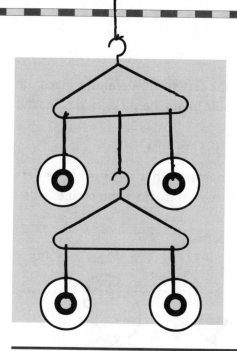

5. Repeat steps 2, 3, and 4 with the second hanger.

6. Tie the second hanger to the first, and hang the mobile near your window so that light bounces off the CDs.

This is just one simple design—see how big and complex you can make your mobile as you collect old CD-ROMs.

 **CD-ROM Coasters**

Here's a gift for your parents or a friend. Coasters are placed under beverage glasses so they don't stain or leave a water ring on the table. If your parents ask you not to put a glass or a soda can down on their favorite table, here's a solution that is fun and works.

MATERIALS

- Some old CD-ROMs (Remember to make sure your parents will never want to use them again.)
- Adhesive felt sheets (Look for these in craft stores. One side is felt and the other side is very sticky.)
- Scissors

DIRECTIONS

1. Peel off the backing of the felt sheet. Carefully place the CD-ROM with the picture side up on the sticky side of the felt sheet.

2. Trim away the felt around the CD-ROM.

You now have a CD-ROM coaster with a felt surface underneath. The felt will keep the coaster from sliding on the table.

SOFTWARE

THE BEST COMPUTER on the planet is only as useful as the programs that it runs. A **program,** or **software,** is a list of very detailed instructions telling the computer what to do. Software can be anything from an entire operating system, such as Windows, to a simple game like Tetris.

Why is software called soft?

Software is called soft to distinguish it from hardware, or the actual computer. Hardware is something that you can touch, while software is information.

Hard-wear   **Soft-wear**

What commands does my computer know?

The CPU, or central processing unit, that comes with your computer knows only a few basic instructions—simple things like ADD, SUBTRACT, MULTIPLY, and DIVIDE. It also knows how to compare two numbers. If we were to ask the computer if 5 is more than 6, it would say no, it is not.

In the early days, the only kind of instructions that computers understood were those that looked like secret code—all numbers. The computer might understand that instruction #1 meant "Add two numbers together," while instruction #42 meant "Compare two numbers and answer yes if the first is more than the second."

Since computers use only 1s and 0s, do programmers have to use these numbers too?

No. Most modern computers count in what is called "Base 16"; they count as 1, 2, 3, 4, 5, 6, 7, 8, 9, A, B, C, D, E, F, 10, and so on.

Early computer programmers had to think and count in Base 16 to write any program. Now programmers can use normal Base 10 numbers, and the computer converts them into what it needs all by itself.

I have seen programs printed out on paper, and the words looked like English. Can computers really understand plain English?

Modern programmers can use words instead of numbers because of something called a programming language. A **programming language** is really just a collection of commands, in English, that the computer translates into its own language to perform an action. Commands are always in capital letters—like ADD, SUBTRACT, and so on. Programmers need to be sure commands are all in the right order, or an entire program will be messed up.

What are the different programming languages?

BASIC

One common programming language for beginners is called BASIC, but it is not used on many modern computers—only older PCs. *BASIC* stands for Beginner's All-Purpose Symbolic Instruction Code. What a mouthful! John Kemeney and Thomas Kurtz at Dartmouth College designed it in the 1960s. Its purpose was to be a simple language that anyone could use to solve problems; practically every programmer learns how to write his or her first computer program with BASIC.

Visual BASIC

Visual BASIC is a computer language used to create all the visual things you see in Windows programs, such as onscreen buttons to click, text boxes, windows, and labels. As you program with this language, you can create a button that tells the program to do something when someone clicks on the button.

COBOL

COBOL, also known as Common Business Oriented Language, was designed so you could write programs using words rather than numbers. COBOL was invented by naval officer Grace Hopper in the mid-1960s (she later became an admiral).

Many COBOL programmers are now busy fixing problems with the clocks in computers that still use COBOL. Most of the problems are in computers from the 1960s and 1970s with small memory chips that had room to store only the last two digits of the year. A computer programmed in COBOL will think a date printed as 01/12/00 is the year 1900 instead of the year 2000.

Pascal

Pascal was created to teach the basics of computer programming to students. Niklaus Wirth made up this language and named it after the seventeenth-century French mathematician Blaise Pascal, who built one of the earliest mechanical calculating machines. These days scientists use Pascal to help solve complex problems.

Is BASIC easy to use?

Sure!

The first command to learn is PRINT. Commands are always written in capital letters. PRINT is used to display something on the screen. For example, if we typed the command PRINT "HELLO," the computer would respond by printing HELLO on the screen.

When you want the computer to follow more than one command, you need a way to tell the computer the order in which to follow the commands. In BASIC you do this by numbering the lines, like this:

```
10 PRINT "HELLO"
20 PRINT "BYE"
```

To have the computer start going through all of your commands, you would type RUN. When you run the program above, the computer would print HELLO, then print BYE. (See the box on this page for a longer program you can do yourself.)

BASIC PROGRAM

Here is a simple program written in BASIC. It should work on any computer that can understand BASIC. As you read the program, look for lines that have the command REM at the beginning. These are REMarks, or notes, that a programmer can place in a program to make it easier for other people to read. The computer ignores any line that starts with REM.

So, let's begin. This program will ask you for your name and your birthday and then tell you how old you are.

Every line starts with a line number, which tells the computer the order in which to run the lines.

```
10 REM    ********************************
20 REM    A simple BASIC Program
30 REM    Copyright 1998 by the CompuDudes
40 REM    ********************************
```

These remarks are just to let someone who is reading the program know who wrote it and when. You should always look for remarks when you are trying to figure out what a program does. And if you are writing programs, please use remarks to tell others what you are doing.

```
50 INPUT "Please type your name and press ENTER", A$
```

The command *INPUT* is used to ask the user for information, like a name, a number, or just about anything. The words inside the quotation marks (" ") are a message that the computer will show on the screen to let the user know what to do.

The A$ at the end of the line is called a **variable**, or a place to store information. The letter *A* represents the place where the computer will store the name that the user typed in. The *$* after the *A* tells the computer that the data will be a "string" of letters.

```
60 PRINT "Hello, ", A$
```

This line uses the **PRINT** command to write *Hello* and whatever the user typed back in line 50.

```
70 INPUT "What year were you born?", Y
```

Can you tell what this line does? Just like line 50, it asks the user for some information, the year the user was born. The computer will store the answer in a place called *Y*.

```
80 INPUT "What year is it now?", N
```

Here we do the same thing, but get another piece of information that we need.

```
90 AGE = N - Y
```

Now here is something new. We are using more than one letter for a variable. In line 90, the computer will subtract the year the user was born from the current year, and put the answer in a variable called AGE.

```
100 PRINT "Did you know that you are ",AGE,"years
old",A$,"?"
```

Line 100 prints out a complicated message. Can you guess what it will say?

Here is the whole program, without our descriptions.

```
10 REM      ********************************
20 REM      A simple BASIC Program
30 REM      Copyright 1998 by the CompuDudes
40 REM      ********************************
50 INPUT "Please type your name and press ENTER", A$
60 PRINT "Hello, ", A$
70 INPUT "What year were you born?", Y
80 INPUT "What year is it now?", N
90 AGE = N - Y
100 PRINT "Did you know that you are ",AGE,"years
old",A$,"?"
```

And here is what you would see if you ran this program. The words in *italics* are what the user types in.

```
Please type your name and press ENTER CompuDudes
Hello, CompuDudes
What year were you born? 1989
What year is it now? 1998
Did you know that you are 9 years old CompuDudes?
```

This program could be made better by using the computer's clock to fill in the current year. If you are interested, why not try? As a hint, look at the DATE$ command in a BASIC manual. Are there any other things that you think this program should do?

What is BIOS?

BIOS stands for Basic Input/Output System. It's a set of programmed instructions stored on a chip called the BIOS chip. The instructions are the first thing the computer will look at when it's turned on. BIOS lets the computer know that it has a hard drive, how big the hard drive is, what other drives it has, what ports it has to plug things into, and that it has a mouse and a keyboard.

What is an operating system, or OS?

An **operating system** like Windows or Macintosh is a software program that tells the computer how to do the most basic things it has to do to function, such as loading programs, storing them, running them, and moving data to all the pieces of the computer and the computer's memory. For a computer to work, the operating system has to be stored on the hard drive. Each time the computer is turned on, or restarted, the operating system is loaded from the hard disk and stored in memory chips.

What is a bug?

A **bug** in a program is a mistake. If you were typing in a program in BASIC, and misspelled PRINT, you would have created a bug! This type of bug is called a **syntax error,** and the computer would catch it when you tried to run the program. You would see the error, correct your typing, and try again. Fixing a bug is called debugging.

A bug in a program that you bought from someone else is more likely to be a mistake in planning or a **logical error.** An example of this kind of bug is when your game crashes every time you get a score of more than one million. This happens because the programmer forgot to tell the computer to use enough memory to hold such a big number. This error really happens from time to time.

BETA TESTING

When computer programs are created, they go through a lot of testing before you buy the finished copy in the store. The different stages of testing are named after the first two letters of the Greek alphabet. The first try is called the **alpha** stage, and it usually has a lot of bugs in it. The second try is called the **beta** stage. Many companies go through even more stages (beta 2, beta 3, and so on) until they have a program with all the bugs taken out.

You may be using a beta copy of a hot new computer game right now. Many computer game companies are now making their beta copies available on their Web sites. Why? First, they want to get people excited about the new software. Second, they can get thousands of people to help them test the program for bugs, saving the company time and money.

But bugs can be frustrating, and they can cause problems with the rest of your computer. So before you load a beta copy of a new game, check with your parents.

What should I do if I find a bug in a program I bought?

Ask your parents to call the company customer service or technical service phone number, which you can find in the game manual or on the company's Web site. If the program doesn't work, the company should either send you another copy free of charge or give you your money back.

What is a virus?

A **computer virus** is a program created by someone who wants to hurt other people's computers. Viruses are programs that tell your computer to do something destructive if you, for example, start your word-processing program. It may keep you from starting your computer, or it may delete all of your documents. Why would someone want to do this? Sometimes it's just because someone thinks it's fun or a challenge, but a lot of times it's because the person has a grudge against another person or company, or even against a whole community of computer users. Creating a virus is a serious crime. Many virus makers have been caught and sent to jail.

The biggest problem with computer viruses is that once they are let loose they can travel everywhere—through the Internet and on floppy disks and to and from hard drives. Just like a cold, computer viruses are easy to get and hard to stop. You never know you have a virus on your computer and disks until it does something bad to your computer. To help keep viruses off your computer, you should use antivirus software to scan your computer's hard drive and any floppy disks you put into the computer. (See the next question.)

What is antivirus software, and how does it work?

The good guys of the computer world are creating antivirus programs that can find viruses and stop them from doing bad things to your computer. They make software designed to look for and disable all known viruses. But since about a hundred new viruses are created every month, it's hard for the good guys to keep up with them all.

When you buy an antivirus program, such as McAffee or Norton Anti-Virus, it has a huge list of viruses to look for, but you need to keep it updated. With some help from your parents, you can go to the company Web site every month and download the files that deal with the new viruses. Keeping your antivirus program updated and telling it to scan the hard drive every couple of weeks and floppy disks all the time will keep your computer safe.

Why won't my Mac programs run on my friend's Windows PC?

Macs and PCs use very different CPU chips. This is why they need their own version of any software. Asking your friend's PC to follow your Mac program is like asking you to follow instructions in German (assuming you don't know German!).

Most programs written for one type of computer are available in a version for the other type. If you go to a computer store, you will see that many of your favorite programs have both the Mac and PC versions on the same CD-ROM. These are called **hybrid disks.**

There are two programs, SoftWindows and Virtual PC, that allow a Mac computer to run PC programs. The only problem is that it takes the Mac CPU time to translate the instructions, so the PC programs run more slowly on a Mac than on a PC.

What does loading software mean?

When you get a new game or other software, you have to put it on your computer's hard drive. This is called **loading.** To do this, you put the disk or the CD-ROM in the drive and tell the computer to run the setup program.

The computer moves all the pieces of the program from the disk and stores them on your computer's hard drive (assuming you have enough storage space on the hard drive). Some CD-ROM programs are so large that they load only a small part of the program onto the hard disk. They run from the CD-ROM in the drive. To **download** a program from a Web site means that your computer is receiving a file from another computer through the Internet. Whenever you download a file, be sure to scan it for viruses.

What is shareware?

Shareware is a computer program that is made available for anyone to use for free. There are many free programs available on Web sites. (See the box on the next page for some great sites to try to find shareware.)

There may be problems with loading shareware on your computer. The programs can take a while to download, and they may contain bugs.

Sometimes they even have computer viruses. If you download shareware, be sure to scan it for viruses with an antivirus software program before you run it.

FIND SHAREWARE ONLINE

Here are two of the safest places to find good shareware programs.

http://www.shareware.com

At this site you can find a lot of free games, and software that will run on new Macs and PCs as well as older computers like DOS-based computers, Atari computers, and Amiga computers.

http://www.hotfiles.com/index.html

This Web site is run by one of the biggest computer publishers, Ziff-Davis, and has a lot of safe and tested free software.

Where can I get free software?

You can find free software on Web sites (see the next chapter, on the Internet). Sometimes you can get it in the mail as a demonstration program. You might be tempted to copy a program from a friend, but don't forget that it's illegal to copy software that isn't specifically designed as shareware.

What do the version numbers on software mean?

Companies are always finding ways to improve on successful software programs. When they are happy with a certain set of improvements, they release a new version of the program and give it a number. The first version is always number 1.0. After that, there can be no end to the possible version numbers. Increasing a full version number (from 1.0 to 2.0, for example) usually indicates a major change. Increasing the number after the decimal point (such as from 1.2 to 1.3) means fewer changes. Some companies take this to extremes and have versions like "Version 7.5.1.1." Earlier versions often can't do as many things as later versions, but the fact that a new version of the software is out doesn't mean that the older software won't work. Before you get the next version, check to see if you really need the new features it includes.

What is a word-processing program?

A word-processing program lets you create reports, letters, or anything else that involves typing your ideas into words. Unlike old-fashioned typing, however, once you get your ideas typed into a word-processing program, you can easily make changes. You can correct your spelling (most programs have a spellchecker that will tell you that you've spelled something wrong), you can move blocks of text around, and you can change how the words look on the page. For example, you can change the **font,** which is the style of letters:

This is how the Times Roman font looks in bold type:
This is a font.

This is how the Alleycat font looks in bold type:
This is a font.

You can change the size of the letters and change where the words appear on the page. Some word-processing software lets you change the color of the letters, and some will let you insert graphics. When you are all finished creating a document, you can print your creation on your printer.

What is a spreadsheet program?

Spreadsheet programs like Microsoft Excel are used to collect many numbers and arrange them in different ways. They can also automatically add, subtract, multiply, or divide the numbers. For example, if you have a paper route and you also cut lawns to earn extra money, you might want to keep track of what you earn for each job each month. You can set up columns for each job and each month and record the amount of money you earned. You can then have the computer add up the columns for each type of job each month and then add the columns together to see how much you earned with all your hard work. The program can also easily show you detailed information, like how much Mr. Jones paid for both the paper and lawn work last year, or how much you made for lawn work in July compared to in February.

GAME TIPS

There are so many games that it's hard to give tips for every game, but we have some useful suggestions that can be applied to many games.

Adventure games, where you have to find clues, usually have a limited number of places to find everything, so click everywhere. Adventure games often have you travel from one place to another, sometimes in a maze. Take out a piece of paper and draw a map as you move (some games have a map function—make sure to use it). This will help you to see where you have been and where you have left in the maze to go. Some adventure games, such as LucasArts Dark Forces, have a built-in automatic map that guides you through the mazes.

If you are fed up and can't get past a level, look on the software company's Web site, a game magazine's Web site, or an online game player's forum to discover hints and clues. Your friends at school may also be a source of free hints and tips. Printed magazines can provide the same information, but they can be more expensive. Look online first if you can.

Some game magazines we suggest looking at are:

Next Generation Magazine, at http://www.next-generation.com

PC Gamer Magazine, at http://www.pcgamer.com

Game Revolution, at http://www.game-revolution.com

How long does it take to program a Nintendo game?

➡️ It can take a team of programmers and testers anywhere from six months to a couple of years to produce a great game.

Can I program a computer to do my homework?

➡️ Yes, you can. For example, you could create a program that will compute math problems. Of course, you have to know what kind of math you want to do; you also need to know programming really well. It's probably easier just to do the homework yourself.

You still can't program a computer to write your papers for history or English class. Computers can't think on their own. They require you to use your brain and ideas.

GARBAGE IN, GARBAGE OUT

You may think that computers can never give wrong answers, but they can. If you give the computer the wrong data, it will give you the wrong answer. This is known as "garbage in, garbage out." A computer is not able to tell you that the data you give it is incorrect.

THE INTERNET

THE INTERNET has become a new way to see the world. You can visit castles and museums, and possibly learn something new from someone who is very different from you without ever leaving your hometown.

We do want to caution you about the Internet, though. Don't ever give out your address or plan to meet a stranger in person. If someone sends you a message that seems strange, tell your parents. The best way to surf the Net is as a family whenever possible.

And as always when something is new in the computer world, there are plenty of questions to go along with it. Here are just a few of the questions we most frequently hear about the Internet.

What is the Internet?

Back in the 1960s, when computers were still used mainly by a few scientists and the United States government, there was no way for people to share information between computers. So the Department of Defense created a computer network called DARPANET. It connected the computers of the department together by phone wire.

DARPANET grew. Soon, colleges wanted to be connected to the network. They created their own little college networks, and then connected those little networks to DARPANET. After a while, the network connected colleges and the government across the United States. This network of networks was called the Internet.

The Internet today is getting more complex every minute. More and more people are connecting to it, creating a worldwide community. As of the publishing of this book, it is estimated that about forty-five million people in the United States use the Internet. Every day thousands more go online for the first time.

The Parts of a Small Portion of the Internet

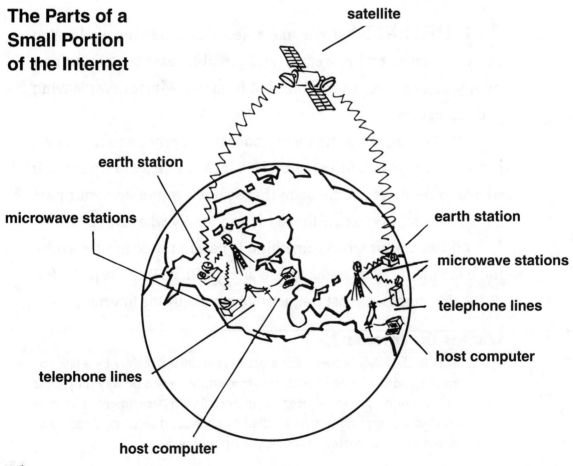

satellite

earth station

microwave stations

earth station

microwave stations

telephone lines

host computer

telephone lines

host computer

What is the World Wide Web?

The World Wide Web is part of the Internet. It allows you to experience the Internet in pictures, video, sound, and graphics—not just in words and numbers. When people used the Internet in the 1960s, all they saw were letters and numbers—no pictures.

In 1989 Dr. Tim Berners-Lee from England created what we now call the World Wide Web. He thought that people should be able to share all of their knowledge and also be able to see it in pictures, anywhere in the world. In 1991, the World Wide Web was introduced to the world.

Since then millions of Web sites have been created, and thousands more are put on the Web every day. Thanks to Dr. Berners-Lee's invention, you can find information about practically anything from nearly anywhere in the world.

Who else is connected to the Internet?

People from all over the world, from Europe to Australia to the South Pole, are connected to the Internet. Your friends, members of your family, and your teachers may be part of this growing community. The best way to find out about it is to get online yourself!

What do I need in order to get on the Internet?

Your computer should have a color monitor, a mouse, and at least two gigabytes of hard drive space. You need a fast computer (at least a 486) and at least 16 megabytes of RAM.

You also need a modem. These days a modem that is as fast as or faster than 28.8 bps is best. (*Bps* means bits per second and refers to how much data can be transmitted to and from your computer in one second.) You will also need your parents' help to connect the phone wire to the wall phone jack. They might want to get a second phone line if you are going to use the Internet a lot.

Finally, you'll need a company to give you access to the Internet. Companies like America Online, Prodigy, and the Microsoft Network offer their own content, like games, news, and kids-only areas, in addition to

Internet access. An Internet service provider, also called an ISP, provides only access to the Internet. When you sign up with one of these companies, you will receive software called a Web browser so you can see the Web sites on your computer.

What is a cable modem?

A cable modem works the same way as a telephone modem, but it is about ten times faster. That's because it gets hooked up to the same cable that is used for your cable TV. The information travels faster through this kind of cable, called fiber-optic cable. In a **fiber-optic cable,** which is made of glass fibers, information travels in the form of light beams instead of electricity. Not everyone has a cable modem, because it would require your cable company to replace the old **coaxial cable** with the fiber-optic cable, which costs millions of dollars and takes months to do. The coaxial cable is made of aluminum and copper, and information goes through it more slowly than it does through fiber-optic cable. Information travels at the speed of light through fiber-optic cable—there is no electricity, just light pulses. If you are in a neighborhood with new fiber-optic cable, you can probably get a cable modem. The cost is generally around $90 to install the modem and wire in your house. High-speed Internet service costs anywhere from $30 to $40 per month.

What is the difference between a Web page and a Web site?

A Web page is one screen of information in a Web site. A Web site is a collection of Web pages on the World Wide Web. Some Web sites have hundreds of pages. Sometimes people call the Web site name a Web site address.

What do all the letters in a Web site address mean?

Here's one example, the Web site address of the CompuDudes:

```
http://www.compududes.com
```

The http:// is short for "hyper text transfer protocol." This is used to let other computers know that the letters after it will be a Web site address.

The www stands for World Wide Web and tells the computer that you are looking for a Web site. The compududes is the name of the company you are looking for. The .com tells the computer that you are looking for a commercial Web site. Addresses that end in .org indicate nonprofit organizations. Ones that end in .gov are U.S. government Web site addresses. Address that end in .edu are colleges or universities.

CREATE YOUR OWN FAMILY WEB SITE

These days everyone seems to have a Web site. Your school may have one, and maybe your friends do too. It's very easy to make your own. America Online, Prodigy, and CompuServe let you make your own family Web pages on their services, and they also let you publish your site on their systems. For kids, Microsoft's Creative Writer is an excellent program that lets you design and create your own Web page. You can easily publish your Web site on online services like CompuServe, or on an Internet service provider like AT&T World Net.

If you want to make a better Web site and use software that is more advanced than the simple Web-development technology available on America Online, then look for the following software: Microsoft Front Page, Adobe Pagemill, or Macromedia Dreamweaver.

These programs will lead you step by step through designing a basic Web site. You don't have to know any programming languages, but if you learn HTML (hypertext markup language, the programming language for Web sites), you can use it with these programs. If you want to add photographs, you may need to look for software called clip art. Clip art refers to pictures and photographs that are free to use. It can be bought as software, or it can be downloaded from the Internet.

Why does the Internet seem so slow?

The information and graphics on the Internet are made up of lots of bits. Each bit has to be transferred through telephone wires and your modem. The phone line carrying sound cannot send information faster than 56,000 bits per second because it is made out of four thin copper wires. The physical parts of the Internet are old. Most of it is still made up of these thin copper wires. If you live in an area where the phone wires have been improved by the addition of fiber-optic cable, then you may get connected at a faster speed during certain times of the week. Eventually things will get faster for everyone on the Net as the connections are improved (see Chapter 5 for more about what's in store for the Internet).

Where is my modem calling when I log on?

Your modem is calling the computer where your online company is located. Your computer calls a local number in your neighborhood and then is automatically connected to the company's computer far away so your parents only have to pay for a local phone call. For example, America Online's computers are in Vienna, Virginia. If you and your folks are Web surfing, you could be connected to any computer in the world—from Australia to Los Angeles, California.

Why does my modem make a screeching noise when I log on to the Internet?

The noise you hear is the sound of your modem communicating with the modem at the other end of the phone line. Modems do all of their communication with sound. You hear only the part when the modems first connect. Basically, your modem is saying "Can you hear me?" to the other modem.

What is a Web browser?

A Web browser is a program that helps you get around on the Internet. Without a browser you could get around only by knowing a Web site's exact address. With a browser, you can do just that—browse from site to site. Two popular browsers are Netscape and Microsoft Internet Explorer. America Online and CompuServe have their own built-in browsers, or you can choose to use Explorer or Netscape. All browsers have onscreen buttons like "Back," "Forward," and "Favorites," or "Bookmarks" (where you can list your favorite Web sites). Browsers can also "remember" which Web sites you often visit. If you type in www.a, the browser will finish typing www.apple.com if you visit the Apple Web site often. You can also send and receive email through a browser if you are using an Internet service provider.

INTERNET SCAVENGER HUNT

In a scavenger hunt, you follow clues to find things. The person who finds the most things on the list is the winner.

How can you make your own Internet scavenger hunt? It's easy. It just takes some time and maybe some Web site lists. First, look up some Web sites using either a search engine, such as Yahoo, or a magazine that lists fun Web sites (such as *FamilyPC* and *HomePC*). Look for unusual facts or bits of information on each Web site, and try to make a question using the facts you find. Type or write the question and leave a blank space for the scavenger hunter to fill in the answer (make sure you write the answers down and hide them until the scavenger hunt is over).

Here is an example of some Internet scavenger hunt questions that can take you far and wide.

1. According to the Weather Channel Web site at http://www.weather.com, what is the weather going to be tomorrow in your hometown?

2. At the Web site http://www.castlewales.com/home.html, who is the guide?

3. Find the answer to these questions at the White House Web site, `http://www.whitehouse.gov`.

   What animal is the guide for the Kids' Area?

   What pet did President Harrison keep at the White House?

4. Visit the Disney Web site at `http://www.disney.com` and name some of the rides found in the Magic Kingdom.

5. At the Smithsonian Institution Museum site, `http://www.si.edu`, click around to find the National Air & Space Museum. Find the years the Ranger spacecraft were launched to the moon.

6. Check out the famous outdoor store L. L. Bean at `www.llbean.com`. In what town in the state of Maine can you find the company?

7. Travel far and visit the city of Moscow in Russia at `http://www.moscow-guide.ru`. Name two favorite Russian soups served in restaurants there.

8. At the comic strip "Peanuts" Web site, `http://www.unitedmedia.com/comics/peanuts`, find out who is the cartoonist who draws the characters.

What does it mean to "log on"?

When you connect to the Internet through an online service, the computer will first ask you to "log on." To "log on" is to let the computer know that you, the user, are ready to connect. If the computer doesn't recognize you as someone who is authorized to access it, it won't let you log on. Most of the time you will also have to type in your secret password. This is a word that you picked the first time you logged on to that computer.

What is a good password?

A good password is one that you can remember but that is *not* your name, the name of your pet, relative, or anything else that is obviously related to you. Good passwords mix random letters and numbers together like:

CX8Y67T   or   5TY7893C

(But please don't use one of these passwords! Anyone reading this book might guess that you chose it.)

Most important, never ever tell your secret password to anyone. Even if they say they are the president of America Online, CompuServe, or Prodigy. No one should be asking you for your password.

My parents put a program on the computer called Surf Watch or Net Nanny. Why is it there?

Parents want to keep you safe when you surf the Internet. These special programs prevent you from going to Web sites that are for adults only.

PLAN A FAMILY TRIP ON THE INTERNET

Are you going on a vacation this summer? There are hundreds of Web sites out there to help you plan your trip. Here are some suggestions of sites to help you plan a basic trip online if you are traveling by car.

First, you can check the Weather Channel, at `http://www.weather.com/twc/homepage.twc`**. Local and international five-day forecasts as well as full-color weather maps can be found on the site. All the information you see on the Weather Channel on TV is there and more.**

If you want to find a list of all the weather sites online, go to `http://www.yahoo.com` **and type in the word *weather*. You'll find sites that give more weather information than you could possibly use. After surfing all those, there will be no excuse for forgetting the umbrella.**

Need directions? Visit `http://www.delorme.com/CyberMaps/` for free information. With the Cyber Atlas, you can get a general map of the city you are traveling to and point-to-point directions. Or click on the Cyber Router for directions. Simply enter your location and your destination, whether you want to go the quickest or shortest route, and the speed your car will be traveling.

Another great Web site for maps can be found at `http://www.mapquest.com`. Here you can find directions from your house to anywhere in the world in any country. Just type in where you are and where you want to go. The Web site will then give you printed directions and a map that you can zoom in on to see more details. You can also find out about interesting places along the way by clicking on links to other Web sites.

Suppose you want to travel by train. Go to the Amtrak Web site, `http://www.amtrak.com/`.

Or how about sitting back and letting someone else drive? Try Greyhound Lines for bus routes and schedules: `http://www.greyhound.com/index.html`.

If you and your family want to find airplane tickets, try looking at any of these airline Web sites:

American Airlines	`http://www.americanair.com`
British Airways	`http://www.british-airways.com`
Canada Airlines International	`http://www.cdair.com`
Continental Airlines	`http://www.flycontinental.com`
Northwest Airlines	`http://www.nwa.com`
Southwest Airlines	`http://www.iflyswa.com`
Trans World Airlines	`http://www.twa.com`
US Airways:	`http://www.usairways.com`
United Airlines	`http://www.ual.com`

Once you get there, where are you going to stay? Head over to this site, which lists more than eight thousand hotels around the world, including all the major hotel chains: `http://www.all-hotels.com`.

To get around, you might need a car. The Internet has that covered—visit these sites:

National	`http://www.nationalcar.com`
Budget	`http://www.budgetrentacar.com`
Avis	`http://www.avis.com`
Hertz	`http://www.hertz.com`

If you are looking for United States national parks, go no further than the National Park Service Site, at `http://www.nps.gov`. The site includes links to all of the national parks, directions, phone numbers, and also information about special permits and safety precautions you should be aware of before visiting the parks.

Among the most popular resorts in the United States are the Walt Disney theme parks. At `http://www.disney.com` you will find links to parks in the United States and other Disney attractions, including Euro Disney in France and the Disney Cruise Line. Everything you need to know is here, including pictures of rooms in every hotel and camera shots of all the parks.

And how about a really out-of-this-world vacation? Take a look at the U.S. Space Camp Web site, `http://www.spacecamp.com`. There you learn about all the programs that this unique training center has to offer budding astronauts.

Can you stay online too long?

It's easy to get so involved in the Internet that time slips by without your realizing it. If your eyes are going buggy and it's ten at night, and you haven't finished your homework, then you have been online too long. You also need to watch how long you are online if your parents are paying for the extra time. Even if you have unlimited monthly access, your parents are still paying the phone bill. It's also good to remember that there are other fun things you can do with your time, like playing outside, visiting friends, and just breathing some fresh air! If you easily lose track of time, consider putting a timer next to your computer so it will remind you to log off after twenty minutes.

Is there a "Yellow Pages" for the Internet?

There are several ways to look up Web sites on the Internet. They are called "search engines." Two favorite search engines are Yahoo and AltaVista. To get one of these, simply type in its Web site address (see the box on the next page). Once you are there, you can enter search words that help you look for Web sites.

GET HELP WITH YOUR HOMEWORK

You can use a search engine to look up the answer to just about any homework question by typing in specific words. Or, if you just type in "homework" or "homework helper", you will be directed to sites that can help you with your schoolwork. America Online and Prodigy have homework helper areas in special "kids-only" areas or homework forums. Click away, but remember that the helpers can't do your homework for you.

A search engine is a Web site that lets you search for anything that is listed on the Internet. Here are some popular search engines:

Yahoo	www.yahoo.com
AltaVista	http://www.altavista.digital.com/
Lycos	www.lycos.com
Excite	www.excite.com
Infoseek	www.infoseek.com

All of these search engines allow you to type in key words to search. But remember that a search engine literally searches all the Web sites for the words you type in. If you search for the word *dog,* the search engine will look for every single Web site that has the word *dog* in it. You would get a huge list that includes hot dog companies, dog clubs, dog kennels, and listings of bands with the word *dog* in their name.

You'll need to make your search more specific by adding more key words. For example, if you were looking for information about the famous dog sledding race held in the state of Alaska, you could type "Alaska+dog+sledding+Iditarod." The search engine will then search through its list of Web sites for the sites where all of those words appear. If you are lucky, it won't find that many. The quote marks are important because they tell the search engine to look for everything inside the quotes. The plus signs tell the engine to look for all the words together. Learning what search words to use and what symbols to use will help you learn how to use a search engine. Most search engines have a help file to teach you how to look for information on the Internet.

What are hyperlinks?

Hyperlinks are shortcuts between Internet addresses. A hyperlink can be a word in a paragraph you are reading that is a different color. If you hold your mouse over that word, you should see a hand symbol. If you then click on that word, your computer will open a page with more information on that topic.

What does it mean to download files from the Internet?

To **download** means to move files from someone else's computer to yours. If you send files from your computer to someone else's, that's called **uploading**.

Can I get a computer virus from the Internet?

If someone sends you an email that has what's called an "attachment," and if you download the attachment to your computer's hard drive and start the program, there is a chance you could get a virus.

The best thing to do is never put a program on your computer from the Internet if it comes from someone you don't know. Even if it does come from someone you know, first save the file to a floppy disk, then scan the disk with antivirus software before you open it.

COOL KIDS' WEB SITES

There are many Web sites for kids, more than we could list here. Here are some of the more unusual sites we know of:

Ecola Newsstand Web site: find links here to every newspaper and magazine in the world.

    http://www.ecola.com

At this site you will find a great book that teaches the basics about the Internet.

    http://www.wiley.com/products/subject/children/
    children/sports/gralla.html

The House Rabbit Society — for owners of pet rabbits.

    http://www.rabbit.org

The Astronomy Picture of the Day.

    http://antwrp.gsfc.nasa.gov/avod/astropix.html

Flying Contraptions: a site about things that flew and those that didn't.

    http://www.prysm.net/~jnuts/

Looney Tunes Sound Source: if you want to hear all the sounds of the cartoons.

    http://www.nonstick.com/sounds

Hadrosaurus foulkii: **the first dinosaur skeleton found in North America.**

    http://www.levins.com/dinosaur.html

Learn about Warner Bros. Animation and create your own cartoons.

    http://www.wbanimation.com

Learn how to speak Klingon and hear Klingon spoken at this site!

    http://www.kli.org/KLIhome.html

Check out the Iguana Camera—live!

    http://iguana.images.com/dupecam.html

Or look for the fish with the Fish Camera.

    http://www1.netscape.com/fishcam

Or look for the giraffes at the Cheyenne Mountain Zoo in Colorado.

    http://c.unclone.com/zoocam.html

Golden Gate Railroad Museum Home Page.

    http://www.ggrm.org/

And check out the other great children's books from John Wiley & Sons.

    http://www.wiley.com/products/subject/children/
    children/

What is email?

Email (electronic mail) is mail that you send through a computer rather than with an envelope and a stamp. You need to be connected to the Internet to send and receive email. Most people use the email programs that are found on services like America Online or that come with Internet browser programs like Internet Explorer or Netscape. Email programs ask you to type in the email address of the person who will get your email. Sometimes there is a space to type the subject of the email, and then there is a big space for your message. Most email takes only a few minutes to travel thousands of miles.

What does an email address really mean?

You have probably seen an email address like this one:

`bobsmith@bhf.com`

This is Bob Smith's email address. You can tell that by the first part—`bobsmith`. The @ sign tells you that he is at `bhf`. The last part, `.com`, means that `bhf` is a commercial company. Here are some other email addresses with different endings:

`hari@whitehouse.gov`   Hari gets his or her email at the White House, which is a government address *(gov)*.

`marymm@alt6.5a.mil`   You know that Mary works in the United States military because there is a *mil* at the end of her email address.

What if I get an email that seems strange from someone I don't know?

The best thing to do is to let your parents know and not answer the email. It would help if you print the email and show it to your parents. Your parents should then call or email the company that you use to go online and let them handle the problem.

Can someone else read the email that I send?

Most of the time only the person that you sent the email to can get your message. Most of the email that is sent could be read by someone along the way, but they would have to have access to the computers that send and receive email. Netscape and Internet Explorer browsers allow you to **encrypt,** or make secret, your email before you send it.

What is "snail mail"?

Snail mail is what people now call the mail that travels through the post office. Compared to email, it is as slow as a snail.

What are smileys?

Smileys are symbols that you can add to the end of your email to show how you are feeling. They are made using semicolons, colons, periods, commas, parentheses, and different types of brackets. You can find all of them on your computer keyboard. Try making up your own smileys! Here are some examples:

:-)	This is your basic smiley.
:)	This is a little smiley.
,-)	A winking smiley.
:-(	An unhappy smiley.
:-V	A shouting smiley.
:-#	This means your lips are sealed, or it can mean that you wear braces.
>:-l	This is a Klingon (from *Star Trek*) smiley.
:-"	This means you are whistling.
:-~)	This one means you have a cold with a runny nose.

These symbols can also be added to your email or when you are chatting with someone online.

\<g>	This is a grin.
\<s>	This is a sigh.
LOL	This means "Laughing out loud."
RLOL	This means "Really laughing out loud."
BTW	This means "By the way."
IMHO	This means "In my humble opinion."
BRB	This means "Be right back."

When I am online, we can't use the telephone. What can we do?

If they can, your parents should get another phone line just for the computer. If they can't, remember that when you are using the only phone line to go online, no one can call in or out. Try to keep your connect time to a minimum. For example, you can write your emails offline, then connect only when you are ready to send them. Try to schedule your time online when people aren't as likely to need to use the phone. Make sure everyone in the family knows and agrees to this schedule. If you have "call waiting" on your phone line, be sure to switch it off before you go online because if someone calls in, they can interrupt your connection.

THINK BEFORE YOU WRITE

The messages you send across the Internet can be read the wrong way. You might, for example, write "I can't stand you" to someone as a joke, but without being able to see or hear you, they won't know you are kidding.

When you talk to someone in person, it's easy for them to see when you are just kidding because you will smile at the person when you say something like this. On the Internet you can't see the other person and they can't see you. Be aware of what you say and how you say it so the other person understands what you really mean.

What is a newsgroup?

A **newsgroup** works like a giant electronic bulletin board. Anyone who wants to can post their thoughts on the newsgroup's subject for anyone else to read. You can get to use newsgroups through your Web browser software like Netscape or Microsoft Internet Explorer. You can find a newsgroup for just about any subject you can imagine. Here are some examples:

`alt.kids-talk`	A newsgroup for kids of all ages
`alt.tv.nickelodeon`	A newsgroup dedicated to the cable television network

What is an online forum?

A **forum** is a lot like a newsgroup, but it is a feature of a commercial service like CompuServe or America Online rather than the Internet itself. Usually the topics are filed in folders, and the comments are listed by the date they were added. The number of messages posted in a forum can be infinite, and often the conversation gets away from the original topic.

On America Online look for the "Kids Only" area. Every imaginable topic is talked about in these forums, from homework to games to your favorite television shows.

What is a mailing list?

A mailing list works like this: You find a group or club you want to partici-
pate in and you send an email to be put on a mailing list. When the leader of
the club wants to let the group know something, or perhaps send a monthly
newsletter, you and everyone else on the list will each get email. If you
want to stop getting the email, you have to unsubscribe from the mailing
list. Instructions how to do this are usually included with the email you get.

What is a chat room?

Chat rooms can be found online on Web sites, on America Online, and on
other commercial services. On America Online the Kids Only area has safe
chat rooms, where only kids are allowed to take part in the chat.

The chat room screen is usually blank except for typed messages that
scroll up as new ones are added. Usually the name of the sender shows up
next to that person's message. Each topic in a chat room is called a message "thread," and all the threads "weave" through the chat room to make
one big discussion. Because most chat rooms are very busy, it can be hard
to keep track of where the conversation is going. The best thing to do is to
just read for a while before you jump in.

You have to be careful in chat rooms, though. If anyone starts asking
you personal questions, don't answer them. The leaders of chat rooms usually stop this from happening, but if it does happen, tell your parents and
have them email the forum leaders.

How do I find and download graphics?

There are graphics everywhere on the Internet and a lot of Web sites from
which to download free artwork, but you usually have to have a graphics
program installed on your computer in order to see these pictures. If you
have a program like Microsoft Publisher, which helps you to create banners,
newsletters, and pictures, you can go to the Microsoft Web site and download more graphics that were not included with your software. Companies
that make graphics software, such as Adobe Systems and the Corel
Corporation, also have free graphics you can download as long as you have
the software to open them.

How can I view videos on the Web?

You need special software. There are two very popular programs that you can download for free from the Internet. Most Web sites use one or the other or both.

The first, called Real Audio, is from the Web site `http://www.real.com`. In addition to the graphics program, the Real Audio site lets you see news reports from many places all over the world. There are also many other educational sites that have Real Audio videos.

The other popular video viewer is from Apple Computer and is called QuickTime. It comes as part of many different kinds of software, or you can download it for free from the Apple Web site at `http://www.apple.com`. Much of the video that you find online can be viewed using the QuickTime program.

Is the Internet really dangerous?

In many ways, the Internet is just like real life. You already know all the rules about meeting strangers. The rules are basically the same on the Internet, with a few changes. First, pick a screen name that is not your own name and that is not another boy's or girl's name. Something like "star123" is a good choice. It's okay to talk to new people on the Internet, as long as you don't give them your name, address, phone number, or any other personal information about yourself. But if anyone you are talking to starts acting weird, tell your parents. Never agree to meet in person someone you've talked to over the Internet. If you want to meet another kid who you've talked to, get your parents to arrange it with his or her parents. As in real life, it's safest to go places on the Internet that you know are okay, like the Kids Only area on America Online.

WEB SITES FOR EVERY SPORT

Basketball	http://www.nba.com
Bowling	http://www.pba.org
Car racing	http://www.nascar.com
Football	http://www.nfl.com
Hockey	http://www.nhl.com
Horse racing	http://www.kentuckyderby.com
Golf	http://www.masters.com
	http://www.golfWeb.com
Iditarod dog sledding	http://www.dogsled.com
Rodeo	http://www.prorodeo.com
Running	http://sunsite.unc.edu/drears/running/running.html
	http://www.bostonmarathon.com
	http://www.runnersworld.com
Rugby	http://www.netbenefit.co.uk/rwc95/rwc.html
Sports Illustrated For Kids	http://www.sikids.com
Tennis	http://www.tennisserver.com
Volleyball	http://www.volleyball.org

Will the Internet replace my teacher?

Sorry, but we don't think that will happen. Computers and the Internet are very good resources, but you need to have someone in the classroom who has a lot of experience and knowledge to direct you.

GOOD COMPUTER HABITS

THIS CHAPTER offers advice about how to make your computer more fun and safer to use. Good computer habits, such as backing up your work, are something you should try to practice every day. Most of them are common sense, and you probably do many of these things already. We also talk about computer safety, which means keeping your computer safe from potential damage, as well as keeping *yourself* safe.

What should I do when I am finished with the computer?

Make it a habit to save your work, exit the program you are working with, turn off the computer, and carefully put your floppy disks in a safe spot, such as a box in a desk drawer. Never store your floppy disks next to the computer or the monitor. Information is stored on floppies magnetically, and the computer and the monitor send out a magnetic pulse every time they are turned on. If you were to leave a floppy disk on the computer for several weeks and turn the computer on every day, information on the disk would gradually be deleted.

What's the best way to share a computer with classmates and my family?

At school, your teacher probably has a time set aside when you and your classmates can use the computer. If you find that there are arguments over who gets to use the computers, talk to your teacher about scheduling enough time for everyone.

At home, the best thing to do is to sit down and talk about how your family will use the computer. Decide on a schedule so that everyone gets a chance to use it when they need it. And don't forget to schedule some time to use the computer together so that you can help teach your younger brother to play a game, or surf the Net for cool stuff with your mom and dad.

My eyes get tired from looking at the computer screen for a long time, and my parents want me to stop using the computer. What can I do, and why should I?

When you play with your computer for a long time and stare at the screen, your eyes get tired because they are staring at the same thing (your monitor). If you have a window in the same room with your computer, make sure you stare out the window once in a while. When you look out the window, your eyes get exercised because they focus on things far away.

After an hour you should get away from your computer. Not only do your eyes need a break, but your muscles will also need a stretch, and your lungs will need some fresh air! Remember that there are fun things to do besides using the computer. Your computer will always be there when you get back.

Our computer desk gets real messy. What can we do?

Make sure that you put the floppy disks and CD-ROMs back into their cases. Also make sure the storage box is kept away from the computer. Information is stored on floppy disks magnetically. If you keep the disks near the monitor or the computer, the magnets in the computer and the monitor can destroy the information stored on the disks. If you have a lot of computer manuals, papers, and books, find a shelf to put them on or a box to store them in.

Is it okay to stack paper on top of the monitor, the computer, the cable modem box, or the printer?

No, it's not okay. Your computer and everything attached to it have moving parts, and they also produce a lot of heat. The heat from the monitor, the computer, the cable modem, and the printer is vented from holes on top. If you cover the holes with paper and books, the heat becomes trapped inside the machinery and can damage the electronic parts inside. Make sure that the back of your computer, where the fan is located, is clear and that the computer is not flat against a wall. On most computers, the fan pulls air through the computer to cool it and blows the warm air out the back of the computer.

Under our computer desk there is a real mess of wires. I don't want to bump or move them, because they might be dangerous. What can I do?

After you plug in the speakers, the computer, the monitor, and the printer, plus all the other wires that connect stuff to your computer, your floor looks like it's covered with spaghetti. Loose wires can be a nuisance and a danger. It is a good idea to get the cables and the surge protector off the floor. But don't try to do it yourself. Ask your parents to tie up those loose cords and attach the power strip to the desk or the wall to make things a little neater.

In the summertime we get a lot of lightning in our neighborhood. We always unplug the television—do we need to unplug the computer?

It is a good idea to unplug the computer as well as your TV and the VCR during a storm. Make sure to unplug the phone wire that is attached to the modem too. If you don't, your computer and TV could be zapped by lightning and be permanently damaged. The electricity from the lightning can get into the wires outside your house and travel through your house's electrical wires and phone wires. This extra electricity can damage the delicate components in your computer and other electronic equipment.

What can we do to protect the computer and the television if we are not home during a storm?

You can't always be home when a storm hits, so you should be sure your computer is plugged into something called a **surge protector.** A surge protector is sometimes mistakenly called a power strip, but there is a big difference between the two. A power strip is simply a way to make one electrical outlet into six or eight. A surge protector is designed to stop surges, or sudden increases, of electricity.

A basic surge protector looks like a power strip, but it has a stronger fuse that absorbs a lot more electricity before it burns out. More advanced surge protectors let you protect your modem's phone wire too. Other models are designed for your television so that your TV cable is protected.

The best computer surge protectors have alarms that sound when a surge happens; they also have rechargeable batteries that provide extra power for the computer if your electricity goes out. Some are even designed to close all your programs if you happen to be working on the computer when the power goes out!

Prices range from $90 for a basic surge protector to $200 for a surge protector that has a battery system.

Sometimes, though, nature is a lot more powerful than even the best surge protector.

I don't want to lose my homework if something happens to my hard drive. What should I do?

Repeat after us: "I will always back up my hard drive."

To back up your work means that you copy the files you want to save onto a floppy disk. If your file is bigger than a floppy can store (for most floppies this means 1.44 megabytes), then you should back up to something called a tape drive or a Zip drive. If you don't have one of these in your computer, you may want to ask your parents if they can add one.

After you back up your work, be sure to store your backup disk or tapes in a safe place, like a floppy disk storage box. If something ever goes wrong in the computer, you will have a second copy.

It's a good idea to back up all your files at least once a week.

HI, THERE!

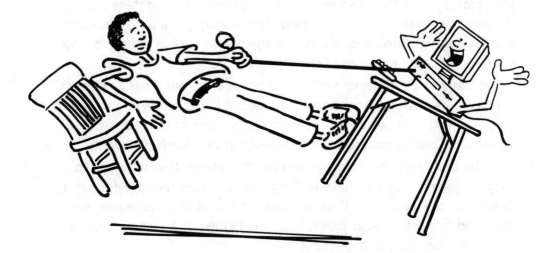

**Someone told me I was shouting in my email.
What does that mean?**

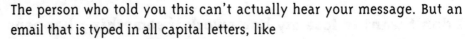 The person who told you this can't actually hear your message. But an email that is typed in all capital letters, like

HI THERE — HOW ARE YOU TODAY?

is considered to be shouting, and, like real shouting, it's considered rude, so don't do it.

**Someone called me a "newbie" on the Internet.
Is he or she making fun of me?**

They might be, but they might be trying to point you to some helpful advice. A **newbie** is just someone who is new to the Internet. Some people who have more experience than you might try to give you a hard time about it, but just ignore them. There are plenty of other newbies like you out there. One good place for you to go as a newbie is the **FAQ** (frequently asked questions) section of any new place you visit on the Internet. That way you can learn about the site without having to ask basic questions that make it obvious you are new.

What is junk email?

Junk email is email that comes to your computer without your asking for it. It's just like all those ads that come in the regular mail. If you get junk email that looks strange, let your parents know so they can help you do something about it.

Most of the time people who send junk email get email addresses by using special software that collects them without permission from either you or the online service.

You can let your online service know that you are getting email you don't want, and they should be able to stop some of it. And you can send email back to the sender and ask them to not send you any more, but that doesn't work all the time.

The good news is that software is on the way that will help you to block a lot of junk email from your online service. Programs from companies like Solid Oak Software, Inc., `http://www.solidoak.com`, are designed to look for certain Web site addresses when you get junk email.

What is the polite way to format an email?

Writing email is just the same as writing a letter with a pen and paper. You should have an introduction like "Dear Paul," or "Dear Natalie." Then you should type some paragraphs that tell your friend something and end by writing what is called a closing, such as "Goodbye," "See you soon," "Take care," or something just as nice before typing your name.

If you are writing to a stranger to find an answer to something, you should politely thank them for taking the time to read your email, and make sure to type your question clearly at the beginning of your email.

When I am on America Online, I can type in information about myself in the Member's Profile area. Should I give my real name and where I live?

It is not a good idea to provide this information on AOL or to anyone on the Internet. It may seem like fun to tell people your name, your age, what city you live in, and what your favorite hobbies are, but there are some bad adults and teenagers who might use this information in a way that could be dangerous to you.

Why do parents get weird about kids using chat rooms?

Parents want to make sure that you have a fun and safe time using the Internet. Chat rooms are not really rooms—they are places where people go to talk about anything. There are separate online chat rooms for adults and for kids. Adults may talk about politics, their jobs, or their children, while kids may talk about their hobbies, their friends, school, vacations, or video games.

Even chat rooms for kids aren't that great because they can use up a lot of time—before you know it, you have been there over an hour. They are also not the best place to have a conversation. Words can sail by faster than you can read them, and unless you are fast at typing, it's hard to keep up. Most chat room visitors spend the first twenty minutes just saying hello to each other!

Email is a better, simpler, and more private way to talk to friends online. It is just as fast, and you can say a lot more.

My parents turned on something called "Parental Controls" on our online service. What is it, and why is it there?

All the online services have this feature. It is designed to keep kids out of adult areas and to keep children safe from everyone else on the Internet.

You may think your parents are not being fair—if so, talk to them about how you feel. You'll learn why they think you need to have these controls on.

Some of the controls stop instant messages from coming to you and can also block any email that is not from friends.

CLEAN YOUR COMPUTER

This may not be your idea of a fun activity, but it is a good thing to do once a month.

Clean that screen!

If your computer monitor screen gets dusty and smudged, then you need to clean the screen. Make sure the monitor is turned off. Using a soft cloth and plain water usually works fine. Lightly wet the cloth (not the screen), and then wipe the screen until it is clean. You don't want to spray the monitor directly, because the fluid can get into the back of the monitor and could damage the electronics inside.

Clean your computer case!

As with cleaning the monitor, you need to lightly dampen a cloth with water. Make sure the computer is turned off. With your parents' help, lightly wipe the vent where the fan is in the back of the computer. When air blows out of the back of the computer, dust can collect there, and if you have a cat, then you might even see cat fur there too.

Clean your mouse or trackball!

If your cursor (the arrow that moves on the screen when you move the mouse) seems to be moving slowly, your mouse may need cleaning. For this you need your parents' help. First, make sure the computer is turned off. Then, open the mouse by spinning the ring located around the ball. Once you loosen the ring, take out the ball and shake out the dust and dirt. If it looks like you can't get all the dirt, you may have to buy a new mouse. They are inexpensive.

Most dirty mice have gotten gunky because they have been used on either fabric pads (the bits of fabric lint are rolled up into the mouse) or a dusty table. So it is a good idea to use only plastic-coated mouse pads, and to keep stuff off the pad. Dust off the pad once in a while too.

Clean the keyboard!

Unless you eat your lunch over your keyboard (which we shouldn't have to tell you is a bad idea), then the most that will be inside is dust and particles of stuff.

Make sure the computer is off, and have your parents help you unplug the keyboard. Get a piece of newspaper and lay it on the kitchen floor to catch the dust as it falls out of the keyboard. Using a hair dryer set on the cool setting, blow the dust onto the paper. You might want to shake the keyboard a few times to remove the dust. To clean the keys, lightly dampen a cloth and gently wipe the keys. When you are through, clean up and have your parents help you plug the keyboard back into the computer.

How do I get peanut butter out of my keyboard?

Well, peanut butter can be tough. You can wipe the keys with a damp cloth, but make sure not to spray anything onto the keyboard. Also, on most keyboards the keys will pop out with a gentle pull. If your keys will pop out, wipe them and click the keys back on. If you really have made a mess that seems as if it will never be clean, you might want your folks to buy a new keyboard (or you might have to buy a new one for them!). Most keyboards are as cheap as $20.

A good way to keep this from happening is to never eat and compute at the same time. Also, if you have younger siblings with sticky fingers, getting a separate keyboard for them is a good idea.

Should I let my baby brother play with the computer?

It's hard to say when is the right time for younger children to start using the computer. That's up to your folks to decide; some parents start children at age three or four. It is always a good idea to supervise your younger brother or sister when they first start using the computer. Pick out a simple piece of software that lets them learn how to click with a mouse. There are good programs for really young kids from companies like The Learning Company and Broderbund.

Mouse.

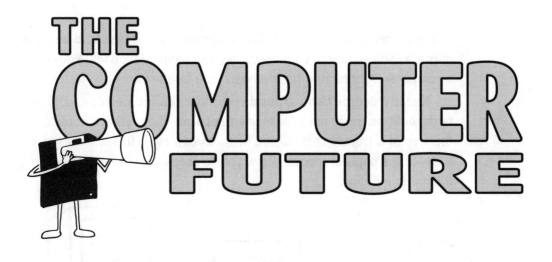

THE COMPUTER FUTURE

THE FUTURE is always hard to predict, especially the future of computers. Some computers that seemed great when they were first made are now long gone for one reason or another, including the Commodore Amiga, the Osborne portable computer, and the first Apple computer laptop computer clone, made by Outbound Systems. Some past predictions about computers now sound pretty ridiculous:

> "I think there is a world market for maybe five computers," from Thomas Watson, chairman of IBM Corporation in the 1940s.

> "Computers in the future may weigh no more than 1.5 tons," from *Popular Mechanics* magazine in 1949.

> "There is no reason anyone would want a computer in their home," from Ken Olson, the founder of Digital Equipment Corporation, in 1977.

We can accurately predict that computers in the future will be smaller, faster, and cheaper. They could end up as a wallet you carry in your pocket. They could be found in every room in your house as screens that start up when you touch them. The keyboard and mouse could be gone. You might be able to talk to your computer and have it talk back. You could have a computer right next to the stereo in your family car.

Already people carry around computers called personal digital assistants, or PDAs. Some are about the size of a small paperback book. Others are the size of a library card. Some of them can even fit inside a wristwatch. Many of the popular models allow you to check your email just by plugging them into a phone.

"So I told the toaster that he didn't know what he was talking about, and he said that he heard it straight from the refrigerator, but then the mixer butted in and said the refrigerator had told her that the coffee maker hadn't said that at all and I said . . ."

We think the Internet will be the one thing that will most change the world we live in. It will be bigger, faster, and far more accessible than it is now.

As we write this book, a few companies are planning to build a worldwide Internet using a satellite network in space. One of these companies, the Teledesic Corporation, is preparing to launch 288 small satellites in low earth orbit by the year 2003. The network would work this way: When you send an email to a friend in France, you will connect to the network from your computer through a high-speed cable modem, which is connected to

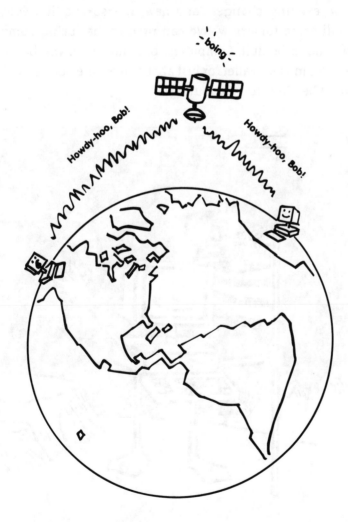

your cable television system or possibly a small home satellite dish. The email is sent to a satellite transmitter, and the message is sent up to the nearest satellite. The message is received and sent to the satellite closest to the area of the world where your message is going. The message would then be sent from the satellite down to the satellite dish in France and then sent to your friend's computer.

You will also be able to see real, nonjumpy video on the Internet (these days the video images are not very good).

In the computer world things are always changing. You can never know what new, exciting changes (and new, not-so-exciting computer headaches) will come tomorrow. We can predict that using computers in the future will never be dull. Computers, big and small, will be everywhere—in your new car, in your wallet, or just about anywhere you can imagine a computer could be. Have fun computing!

Glossary

alpha   Software that has been just completed and is ready for testing.

beta   The second stage of software testing and usually the last stage before it is sold in the store.

binary   A code that is represented by a 1 or a 0. Binary is the basic electronic language that all computers understand.

bit   The smallest unit of information stored in a computer.

bug   A mistake in a computer program. After a program is written, it is "debugged" to find all of the errors and fix them.

byte   A single unit of data stored in a computer. For example, the letter *h* would take up one byte of space on a hard drive.

central processing unit (CPU)   The large computer chip, often called the "brain of the computer," where all of the computations are done to make the computer function.

chat rooms   Places on services like America Online and Web sites around the world where people meet to talk about all kinds of topics.

coaxial cable   A thick cable that connects the television set to the VCR. It is also now used to transmit information through the Internet and into cable modems.

computer virus   A computer program that disrupts or destroys computer data.

cursor   The arrow or bar that moves on the screen when the mouse is moved.

disk   A round piece of plastic or metal coated with magnetic material where all information in a computer is stored.

dot matrix printer   A printer that creates letters by pressing small pins quickly against an ink ribbon.

downloading   The process of getting a computer file from a distant computer onto your home computer.

encrypt   To scramble data into code so that only people who also have the code can read it.

fiber-optic cable   A fiberglass cable that transmits information in the form of light pulses.

flatbed scanner A device with a flat glass surface on which you place documents. The documents are then scanned and copied into your computer.

font A set of characters that have a specific shape and size.

forum A place online to discuss topics with other people.

FAQ Frequently asked questions. These are found on Web sites and answer the common questions that everyone asks about a particular forum's topic.

graphics tablet A flat plastic board connected to the computer that is used to make computer graphics. Using a pen, you can create pictures that will appear on the computer screen.

hamster Nickname for a cordless computer mouse that transmits its position using radio signals.

handheld scanner A scanner that is held in the hand and manually moved over text or pictures.

hardware The computer, mouse, printer, etc., are all hardware.

hybrid disks Usually CD-ROMs that contain programs that can be used on both Apple computers and IBM-compatible computers.

inkjet printer A printer that sprays ink onto paper.

joystick A device that computer game players use to move figures on a screen in computer games.

loading The process of transferring a program from a disk or CD onto your computer.

logical error A programming error that causes a program to create incorrect answers.

newsgroup A type of forum on the Internet that follows a specific topic.

operating system The basic computer program that controls the functions of all parts of a computer system.

phosphor A chemical substance that coats the inside of a computer screen and glows when it is touched by an electron beam.

pixel The smallest spot of light on a computer monitor or television.

program A series of instructions that can be run by a computer.

programming language The code that is used to create software.

random access The ability of a computer to quickly find a specific piece of information within a large amount of information.

scanner A device that transfers an image to a computer.

search engine A program that looks for keywords in a database, Web site, or anyplace online or in the computer where information is stored.

shareware Free software that is distributed by computer programmers.

software Computer programs that make the computer work.

sound card The circuit board in a computer that inputs and outputs sound.

sub woofer A speaker with which lower bass sounds are heard.

surge protector A device that stops surges of electricity from damaging computers and other electronic devices.

syntax error An error in the grammar and spelling used in programming.

track point A pointing device that is a small joystick located between the *G* and *H* keys on laptop keyboards.

uploading The process of sending information from one computer to another.

vacuum tube A glass tube with no air inside. Vacuum tubes are attached to electric wires that can be turned on or off. The first computers, television sets, and radios used vacuum tubes.

variable A place in a computer program where data is stored that can be changed when the computer program runs.

virus See *computer virus*.

Bibliography

Gonick, Larry. *The Cartoon Guide to the Computer.* Harper Perennial, 1991.

Kidwell, Peggy, and Paul Ceruzzi. *Landmarks in Digital Computing: A Smithsonian Pictorial History.* Smithsonian Institution Press, 1994.

Lubar, Steven. *Info Culture: The Smithsonian Book of Information Age Inventions.* Houghton Mifflin, 1993.

Veit, Stan. *Stan Veit's History of the Personal Computer.* WorldComm, 1993.

Index